Who Me? A Superhero

Written by Clara Kennedy Witherspoon

Copyright © 2022
All Rights Reserved

Table of Contents

Dedication i

Acknowledgment ii

About the Author iii

I Wish I Were Never Born 1

Shantika's Gets In Trouble at School 3

Woman in the White Hood 10

The Next day at School 15

The Woman in the White Hood Returns 19

Hardest Lesson to Learn 27

Dedication

This book is dedicated to my loving husband, Ira, who has always believed in my dreams and possibilities.

And to my beautiful daughters, Danielle and Ashley, my pride and joy.

Acknowledgment

In honor of my grandparents, Horace, and Ida Wynn, for raising five resilient women who transferred their determination to persevere and succeed to their daughters. Also, I would like to thank my co-laborers in the counseling profession, Glenda Nnaji (licensed professional therapist) and Tameka Johnson (certified school counselor and instructor). Throughout our friendship, you have been my sounding board.

About the Author

Clara Kennedy Witherspoon was born in Monroe, NC, and educated in the Charlotte - Mecklenburg Schools System. She received a BA degree in Psychology from North Carolina Central University, a Master's degree in Christian Leadership from Liberty University, and the University of the Southwest in School Counseling and School Administration. Mrs. Witherspoon retired from Charlotte Mecklenburg Schools System in January 2022. Her professional career included working in the district as an MTSS Specialist, School Counselor, and Graduation Coach. Clara Witherspoon's belief that we must educate the whole child drove her to create a tool to encourage young girls to identify their self-worth, just like Shantika does in Who me? A Superhero. Also, to encourage educators to look at the whole child when determining the cause of behaviors.

I Wish I Were Never Born

Shantika; Mom called out; where are you? Didn't I tell you to get your lazy behind out of that bed! You better get those dishes washed before leaving this house for school, and I mean it!

Mom said, "That girl gets on my last nerve!" Shantika thought to herself, "I am so tired of being yelled at and having to do everything." Mom screams and yells at me all the time." I can't seem to do anything right. Then, a few minutes later, Shantika's Mom yelled out again, "I don't hear you moving around, don't make me come in there and pull you out of bed!" You know what will happen if I pull you out of bed.

Shantika replied, okay, and said to herself, "I wish I were never born!" I hate this house and Mom. I can't blame Daddy for walking out on her. All she does is scream and yell and say mean things. She never says anything good about daddy or me. She makes me feel worthless, and I know I will never amount to anything! But she doesn't have to keep reminding me.

Move out of the way, said Shantika's Mom. Don't you see me trying to make a cup of coffee?

Girl!; your lazy behind is like your daddy, always in the way.

Shantika thought to herself, "I just want to shrink, or become invisible, so no one can see me or know where I am, thought Shantika !"

Mom shouted out, "Shantika, I am leaving. You need to get Betty Ann over to Ms. Mary's house before leaving for school. Make sure Will gets dressed and ready to go when you leave." "Okay, Mom," Shantika replied and finished her chores before leaving for school.

Shantika's Gets In Trouble at School

"Good morning, Shantika," said her teacher, Ms. Rice. Shantika did not respond and walked straight to her desk, saying, "I don't know why she speaks to me every morning. I know she thinks I am lazy, and she does not like me". I can see it in her eyes.

"Good morning, students said Ms. Rice." Please pull out your homework and place it in the homework basket on my desk. Shantika puts her head down on her desk. Ms. Rice approached Shantika and asked, "did you do your homework?" Shantika replied angrily, no; I didn't! You will get a zero for not turning in your homework, said Ms. Rice. Shantika replied; I don't care!

"Shantika, you will stop talking back to me; as a matter of fact, I will call your Mom, said Ms. Rice." But, Shantika pleaded, no, please don't call my Mom!

I am sorry, Shantika, your disrespect warrants a phone call, said Ms. Rice. Shantika runs out of the classroom. Ms. Rice grabbed her walkie-talkie and called the front office, alerting them that Shantika had run out of the class. The front office secretary replied, Ms. Rice, I will send Mr. Jones, Behavior Modification Technician, to look for her.

Mr. Jones found Shantika hiding behind a door, and he asked; why are you hiding behind a door? Shantika does not answer Mr. Jones. So, Mr. Jones said, Shantika, you need to come from behind the door! No, I am not coming out, replied

Shantika! Mr. Jones frowned, "Shantika, you come out on your own, or I will remove you from behind the door."

Shantika answered, " No, I will not come out!" Okay, Mr. Jones replied, and he removed Shantika from behind the door, picked her up, and carried her to the office. Shantika kicked and yelled, "Put me down!" Mr. Jones took Shantika to the principal's office, where she sat quietly.

Principal Wilson asked Shantika, "what is going on with you?" You arrived at school with a bad attitude. Your teacher shared that she greeted you this morning, and you did not respond. Shantika did not answer Mrs. Wilson. Mrs.

Wilson added, " Okay, Shantika, I will call your Mom." Shantika cried and begged Mrs. Wilson not to call her Mom.

Good morning Ms. Barber. I am Mrs. Wilson, the principal at your daughter's school. Shantika's Mom asked politely, what has she done this time? Well, she ran out of her classroom again, replied Principal Wilson. Would you like to speak with her, said Principal Wilson. Of course, Shantika's Mom responded. Now Shantika, you know I plan to get you when you get home! I am tired of the school calling me about your behavior. So, you better get your butt back in that classroom and stay there. And I will see you after school, she added! Shantika cried and responded, yes, ma'am, and gave the phone back to Principal Wilson.

Thank you, Ms. Barber said, Principal Wilson. I believe the rest of her day will go very well. Shantika looked at Mrs. Wilson with a frown.

Mrs. Wilson called for Mr. Jones to walk Shantika back to her class. "Okay, Shantika," said Mr. Jones, remember what your Mom said, and behave in class. I don't want to have to call your Mom again.

Shantika nodded, slowly walked into her classroom, and sat at her desk. Shantika looked around the room, and her classmates were all staring at her. Finally, she placed her head on her desk.

Ms. Rice looked over at Shantika but decided not to say anything to her, thinking she was not disturbing the entire class or being disrespectful. The school bell rang, and it was time to go home.

Shantika looked up at the clock and felt anxious because she knew what would happen to her when she got home.

"Alright, students, if you ride bus 350, get in the line now," said Ms. Rice. Shantika slowly got into the line. The bus monitor was standing at the door to escort the group of students to the bus lot. Once on the bus, Shantika imagined if she had a different mom, maybe someone famous, like Beyonce or Michelle Obama. Then, she thought, "I know they love their children and don't scream and beat them." Shantika was so deep in her thoughts that she did not realize that her bus had arrived at her stop. Shantika, this is your stop, said the bus driver. Shantika hesitated in getting off the bus, turned, and said goodbye to the bus driver. Then, she looked up, and her Mom was standing at the front door.

Shantika walks past her Mom and enters the house, throwing her book bag on the chair. "Go into your room; you know what will happen", said Shantika's Mom.

Once I finish, you will behave in school tomorrow! A few minutes later, Shantika's Mom walked out of Shantika's bedroom, and Shantika fell on her bed in tears and went off to sleep.

Woman in the White Hood

Around 1:00 AM, a woman clothed in a white hood touched Shantika. Shantika awakened, rubbed her eyes, and realized the person in her room was not her mother.

The woman placed her hand over Shantika's mouth. "I'm the spirit of your PURPOSE", said the woman in a low voice, don't be afraid, Shantika. I am not here to harm you but to show you who you are. Shantika, everyone is given an assignment before being born into the world.

You will learn more about your life and your assignment. Shantika replied, "I don't understand." The woman added, "I know, child, but you will soon understand." Unfortunately, I must leave, but I will be back tomorrow night, and you will begin your journey of truth. Suddenly, the woman in the white hood was gone.

The next night, Shantika lay anxiously in her bed, waiting for the woman in the white hood to show up. Quickly looking at her clock, she realized it was only 10:00 PM. Shantika remembered that the woman in the white did not come until 1:00 AM, so she finally drifted off to sleep. At 1:00 AM, the woman in white lightly touched Shantika and said, "wake up, my child." Shantika opened her eyes and, as always, rubbed them to see clearly. Hi, said Shantika; "I was not sure you were coming back, or even if you were real." But now I know you are, and I did not make you up in my mind, Shantika added. The woman in the white hood responded, yes, child, I am real.

Shantika's First Night Journey

Shantika, hold my hand tightly and close your eyes just as tight. The woman raised their connected hands high in the air and repeated the words, "Before I was born." Next, the woman said, "open your eyes, Shantika, and look around the room."

Do you know any of the people in this room? Yes, my Mom, grandmother, Aunt Barbara, and Aunt Terrie, but I don't see me, said Shantika. You were not born yet, responded the woman in the white hood. Let's move around in the room. They can't see or hear us, she added.

Shantika listened to her Mom talk about how happy she was to be pregnant. She and Raymond had decided to name the baby Shantika, which means something loved, strong, and princess. Shantika's Mom said, "every time I feel her move, the love for this baby overflows." Tears began to stream down Shantika's face, she felt confused and looked over to the woman in the white hood, but the woman in the white hood was staring at a man entering the room. Shantika wiped her tears away and, with a slight smile, said, that is my dad. The woman did not respond but watched the man walk over to Shantika's Mom. Shantika began to watch as well. Shantika's father leaned over, kissed her Mom on her forehead, and sat beside her.

Her dad talked about their plans to build a house before the baby came, and he wanted his new baby girl to have her own home because his parents never owned a home. Shantika kept watching, and she felt so confused about how her life had turned out; she turned and asked the woman in the white hood, "why does my mom hate me so much now?" The woman in the white hood did not respond to her question. Instead, she said, "it's time to leave." Shantika looked up at her, and the woman said, "grab my hand and hold it tight, and close your eyes, only open them this time when I tell you to open them." The woman in white grabbed Shantika's hand and raised their hands high. Then, a few seconds later, she told Shantika to open her eyes. Shantika was back in her bed, and the woman in the white hood was gone.

Shantika snuggled underneath her blanket and quickly drifted off to sleep.

The Next day at School

The next voice she heard was her Mom screaming and yelling for her to get up. Shantika replied, Mom, I am getting out of bed. Shantika's Mom walked over to Shantika's bedroom door and asked, "what did you say?"

Shantika responded, " alright, Mom, I am getting out of bed." With a strange look on her face, Shantika's Mom walked away. "I better get dressed to get the others out to school," said Shantika. Shantika's Mom thought to herself, something is different about that girl, and she continued fixing her coffee. Finally, Shantika gets everyone dressed and fed breakfast. "Okay, Mom, everybody is dressed, had breakfast, and dropped off at Ms. Mary's house. " Shantika's Mom looked up but never said anything. My bus is out there; bye, Mom. Shantika ran out the door to catch her bus.

"Good morning, Ms. Rice," Shantika said. Ms. Rice turned her head and looked directly at Shantika. "Well, good morning, Shantika," replied Ms. Rice. Ms. Rice wondered what was going on with Shantika. She never spoke to anyone. Ms. Rice was preparing to make her regular morning announcement about homework. However,

Shantika was up before she could, placing her work in the homework bin.

Throughout the day, Ms. Rice noticed that Shantika's behavior was different, and she wondered what was causing such a change. Finally, after lunch, Ms. Rice called Shantika to her desk. Shantika, thank you for being the first student to place your homework in the homework bin. I am proud of you because you are having a fantastic day.

Shantika replied, "thank you, Ms. Rice." Ms. Rice then asked Shantika if something special was happening at home. Shantika's eyes opened wide, and she quickly responded, "oh, no, nothing special is happening. Okay, but if you ever need to talk, you can always speak to your school counselor or me. Shantika nodded her head and returned to her desk.

The Woman in the White Hood Returns

Shantika is lying in her bed and struggling to fall asleep. And wondered, was the woman going to return, and did she really visit a period when she was not born? Shantika asked herself, or was the visit a dream? As soon as she asked herself the question, the woman in the white hood appeared. Shantika, your journey was not a mere dream. Shantika responded you are not just a dream! The woman in the white hood replied, no child, I am not. I am Purpose, and tonight you will visit the Wisdom Tree.

Will I see my Mom and dad again? No, responded the woman in white, you will spend time tonight at the root of Wisdom, the woman in white added. Are you ready to go? Shantika replied, I guess. Stand up, give me your hand, and close your eyes, said the woman. While noticing how tall the woman was, Shantika reached her hand to the woman in white, then shut her eyes. The woman in the white raised Shantika's hands, and off they went.

All right, Shantika, you can open your eyes. Shantika looked around; where are we? We are in the land of Wisdom. Do you see the green tree in the middle of the landscape? Shantika responded, yes.

The tree is called a Salab tree, known as the *Wisdom Tree*, said the woman in the white hood. Shantika thought to herself, "that is a strange name for a tree." The woman gestured for Shantika to follow her, moving closer to the tree.

The Wisdom Tree appeared to be just like any old tree, thought Shantika. But the closer she got to the tree, the more she realized that the Wisdom Tree was no ordinary tree. It had eyes and could talk. The woman gently nudged Shantika closer to the tree. The Salab tree spoke, Purpose, who do you have with you this time? The woman responded this is

Shantika. The Salab instructed the woman to bring Shantika closer to him so she could stand in his company.

The Salab tree tells Shantika to gently grab one of his branches and pull it. Shantika reached up and grabbed a branch and pulled gently. The Wisdom Tree directs Shantika to sit upon his roots but don't allow the limb to slip out of her hand. You can call me Wisdom, for I am known as the Wisdom Tree. My roots run deep into the water and connect with the souls that dwell in the world. Do you see the river flowing to your right, asked the Wisdom Tree? Yes, said Shantika.

The Wisdom Tree shared with Shantika, when you touched my branch, I could see your entire life, even before you were born. I know all things, and I also know that "Purpose" took you to a time before you were born. Can you share what you saw when you made your first journey? Yes, said Shantika; I saw my family, Mom, Dad, and aunts. Tell me how you felt when you saw them. Well, first I was excited, then I was sad. The Wisdom Tree then asked, "why were you unhappy?" I was sad because I saw my parents together, they were happy, but now they are not together. What else did you feel?

My Mom was pregnant with me, and she was so excited to be pregnant; Shantika paused. The Wisdom Tree encouraged her to keep talking. My Mom said she loved me, but that is not true. Shantika, "what did you notice about your Dad?" My Dad did love my Mom and me. He said he wanted to build us a house, called me his baby girl, and even kissed my Mom on her forehead.

Wisdom Tree, "I am so confused," said Shantika. The Wisdom Tree asked Shantika, "what would you change if you could change anything about your life?" Shantika responded, first, I would have wanted my Mom and Dad to have stayed together and my Mom to love me for me. And I wish my Mom loved me now the same way she loved me before I was born. What do you think you have learned about both of your parents? They once loved each other and were happy. My Dad was a good man, and my Mom appeared to have been kind. The Wisdom Tree asked Shantika, "why did you say your Mom seemed to be kind?" Well said, Shantika; it's hard for me to think she was ever a nice person and loves us. Although she screams at me, she doesn't spend time with my siblings. She goes to work, yells, and makes me do almost everything.

The Wisdom Tree gestured to Shantika to come closer to the roots of his tree. I am going to share with you some wisdom. I know you are confused and that it is hard for you to imagine who your Mom was before all the unfortunate things happened to your parents. Let me begin with your Dad, who was and is a good man. He loved your Mom and his family very much and did his best to be a good provider. He wanted to provide for his family and build a home, which you heard him say. Your Mom trusted and believed in your Dad, and she thought their lives would have been different.

Shantika asked, "then what happened?" The Wisdom Tree responded that it was not their fault.

The times were different, and your Dad could not find steady work, no matter how hard he tried. Your Mom began to fault your Dad for his inability to provide for his family, although she knew it was not his fault. Your Mom was also doing all she could to take care of you and help to bring in money. Then she became pregnant with your siblings, which placed more of a burden upon your Dad. Your parents started to grow apart and began to fault one another.

What Do I Do?

Shantika, "can you understand?", asked the Wisdom Tree. Shantika replied, " yes," but now that I know what happened, "what do I do?" The Wisdom Tree replied, "what do you think you should do?" I could begin by asking my Mom questions, said Shantika. What questions would you ask your Mom? I don't know said Shantika. The Wisdom Tree shared, "I have listened to the hearts of many souls, and many have set upon my roots. But none understood that the beginning of Wisdom is to listen to their deepest soul.

Shantika asked, "how does a person listen to their deepest soul?" You must look away from your anger and listen to your heart. Your heart will tell you the truth, but you must be willing to accept the facts. "What is your truth, Shantika?", asked the Wisdom Tree. I don't know, said Shantika. Close your eyes, recall your Mom's face, and hear her words, said Wisdom. Shantika opened her eyes wide as if she had seen or heard something. The Wisdom Tree asked, "what did you hear and see?" I saw my Mom crying in her bedroom, and I could listen to her voice, said Shantika. The Wisdom Tree asked, "what did she say?"

She said I am doing my best to keep my family together. I know that I am hard on Shantika, but she is my only help. Shantika began crying. "why are you crying?" said the Wisdom Tree. I have been angry with Mom because she made me help her so that she could go to work and provide for us. I did not understand her; I only knew how I felt and how she treated me, said Shantika. "What do you know now? ",said the Wisdom Tree. I know that my Mom is doing the best she can, she does love me. And although I felt my Mom did not care, she is doing her best, said Shantika. "What have you learned about yourself? " said the Wisdom Tree. I have learned that how I handle my feelings matters.

Hardest Lesson to Learn

"What will you do differently?", said Wisdom. Now that I understand how being angry hurts the people I love and me. I plan to talk about my feelings more, not just keep them inside. Also, I will try and help my Mom more; at least I can do that.

The Wisdom Tree responds; Shantika, you have learned one of the hardest lessons to learn for most: looking beyond your feelings and seeing the truth. Because of that, Shantika, I am giving you a Superpower to elevate your *Purpose*.

Release the branch from your hand, and extend both hands above your head, said the Wisdom Tree.

A golden belt appeared around Shantika's waist, and in the center of the buckler was a picture of the Wisdom Tree. Shantika touched her shiny new belt. The belt is how you will release your Superpower, stated the Wisdom Tree. When you touch the belt, you will change into a Superhero. "*Who Me*? said Shantika," *A Superhero*." Yes, said the Wisdom Tree, you will now be invisible to others unless you choose to show yourself.

In addition, you will have the Wisdom to recognize children in despair. When it is time to use your Superpowers, touch the Wisdom Tree on your belt, said Wisdom.

Purpose returned, Shantika, it is time to go, and although it seems like you have been gone from your home

for a long time, you have not. Okay, said Shantika, and she reached up and hugged the Wisdom Tree.

Shantika looks back at Wisdom and says thank you. Then, Purpose reached for Shantika's hand, and they disappeared.